HOW GOD
SAVES
THE WORLD

Timothy C. Tennent

HOW GOD SAVES THE WORLD

A Short History of Global Christianity

 Seedbed

Printed in the United States of America

Hardcover ISBN: 978-1-62824-373-4
Paperback ISBN: 978-1-62824-369-7
Mobi ISBN: 978-1-62824-370-3
ePub ISBN: 978-1-62824-371-0
uPDF ISBN: 978-1-62824-372-7

Cover design by Strange Last Name
Page design by PerfecType, Nashville, Tennessee

SEEDBED PUBLISHING
Franklin, Tennessee
Seedbed.com

To my dear friends David and Peggy Harvey,
who have embodied God's Unfolding Story
around the world.

Contents

Act Two
The Great Century of Missions, 1792–1910

Act Three
The Flowering of World Christianity, 1910–present

Introduction

Two students, Larry Page and Sergey Brin, sat in their dorm room at Stanford University and pledged themselves to the following mission statement: "To organize the world's information and make it universally accessible and useful." The result was Google, the most powerful and widely used search engine in the world. Today, it seems that large and small businesses are all adopting mission statements. Even businesses with an unambiguous and widely known purpose—such as FedEx, Barnes & Noble, and Nike—all have mission statements. Nike's mission statement, for example, is "to bring inspiration and innovation to every athlete in the world."

The mission craze has even begun to influence the government. Even the U.S. State Department now has a mission statement. Some marriage counselors are now encouraging couples to write up their own personal mission statement. It seems that it is no longer only the church that has a mission. We live in a world awash with mission statements—everybody is on a mission. Clearly the word *mission* has lost its identity as an exclusively Christian term.

This little book is dedicated to helping you understand the mission of the church. It is not easy to tell the story of the worldwide mission of the church of Jesus Christ in such a short little book. Before I became the president of Asbury Theological Seminary, I used to teach a course on the history of missions. I would have the opportunity to spend an entire semester with students and unfold the story over many hours, supplemented by thousands of pages of reading.

I would like to approach this book in a different way. Rather than plowing through countless names and events that make up this remarkable story, I would rather like to invite you out to an evening together. Let's jump in the car and go see a play entitled *God's Unfolding Story*. Like a true epic play, it will be a play in three acts. Another way to envision this little book is to imagine that we decided we didn't want to go out to see a play, but we just wanted to stay home and look at some pictures together. I will throw a picture on the table of some event in Christian history and then tell the story of that picture. We will spend an evening together looking at pictures through the history of the church. Either way, we will look at the pictures or see the play in three acts or three parts. Act 1 will look at the history of missions from the book of Acts until the year 1792. Act 2 will cover the period between 1792 and 1910, and act 3 will look at the history of the church between 1910 and the present.

HOW GOD
SAVES
THE WORLD

Act One

Seven Turning Points in the History of Missions before 1792

Introduction

Ovid, in his *Metamorphoses*, is one of the earliest writers to record the ancient myth of Narcissus. According to Ovid, after Narcissus's encounter with Echo, he fled to a river, where he knelt down to drink. However, as he was about to drink, he caught sight of his own reflection in the water and fell in love. Whenever he tried to drink from the river, the reflection was disturbed. So, Narcissus refused to drink, and he gazed longingly at his own reflection until he died. The myth of Narcissus has been used by modern writers and artists as varied as Keats, Dostoevsky, Freud, and even Bob Dylan to highlight the destructive nature of narcissism. Today, mirrors are among the most common objects in the world. Mirrors are used in telescopes to bring distant images closer. Sometimes mirrors are distorted and twisted and used in carnivals to make us laugh at our own caricatures. Mirrors are used every day by people all over the world to help with personal grooming.

According to Webster's dictionary, a mirror is defined as a smooth surface with spectral qualities. In other words, a good mirror is one that is able to reflect an image with clarity and precision.

Missions history can be conceptualized as a mirror, or image reflector. Just as God in Jesus Christ entered history in order to show us what God was like, so the church is to embody and reflect the very presence of God in the world. In short, missions history is a reflection of the incarnation. The role of the church is not just to bring a particular message, but to *embody* the message as we image the incarnation and foreshadow the coming New Creation. Undoubtedly, numerous examples can be cited where we have distorted God's intention for the church in the world. Like the distorted mirrors at carnivals, we have sometimes reflected only a crude caricature of Jesus Christ in the world. However, God in His providence has chosen and sent the church into the world to bear witness to His glory and the salvation which is found in Jesus Christ.

In act 1, we will explore the earliest period of our Christian history, as the church sought to be faithful in reflecting the glory of Jesus Christ. Act 1 will cover the period from the first century, as recorded in the book of Acts, until the year 1792. We will explore this vast period by looking at seven "snapshots," which cover this period of mission history. It is hoped that these seven pictures will, in some way, reflect something of the vibrancy and beauty of the earliest days of the church in mission in the world.

CHAPTER 1

Unnamed Disciples from Cyprus and Cyrene

The first picture I want to show you is the story of a group of disciples from the island of Cyprus and from a city in North Africa known as Cyrene. You might expect that the first picture we would look at would be the apostle Paul, the reputed "Apostle to the Gentiles" (Rom. 11:13; Gal. 2:8) and probably the greatest missionary in the history of the church. However, I have chosen to focus on a small group of unnamed disciples from Cyprus and Cyrene who were the first to address the gospel to Gentiles who had no prior identity with Judaism. These early missionaries preached the gospel to Gentiles *before* Paul's first missionary journey. They were used by God to foster what is arguably the most important breakthrough in the entire book of Acts.

The book of Acts records that a great persecution broke out against the church in connection with the martyrdom of Stephen (Acts 8:1). This persecution caused a scattering of believers from its base in Jerusalem to such faraway places as Phoenicia, Cyprus, and Antioch (Acts 11:19). These scattered believers, Acts records, went around "spreading the word only among Jews." But, Acts 11:20 records, "some of them, however, men from Cyprus and Cyrene, went to Antioch and began to speak to Greeks also, telling them the good news about the Lord Jesus." The Lord blessed these early missionaries, and "a great number of people believed and turned to the Lord" (v. 21). This is the origin of the church at Antioch, which, some years later, would be the sending church for the apostle Paul's great missionary journeys (Acts 13:1).

There are three very important observations that should be made in reflecting on this early breakthrough among the Gentiles. First, *the encounter between these unnamed Jewish believers and the pagan Gentiles of Antioch was precipitated because of the persecution that broke out in Jerusalem.* While it is not good to overly romanticize persecution, it is nevertheless important to see that God has used persecution throughout mission history to advance His purposes.

Second, *we do not even know the names of these believers.* We only know that they were men from Cyprus and Cyrene. These men were not apostles. They were not part of the inner circle of Peter, James, and John in Jerusalem. They occupied the *margins* of the fledgling Christian movement. After the dramatic Gentile breakthrough occurred in Antioch, "news of this reached the ears of the church at Jerusalem" (Acts 11:22). The church leadership was in Jerusalem, while the front edge of God's work was taking place in Antioch. Throughout the history of missions we discover that God often moves from the margins, not from the center of the Christian movement.

Third, *it is the Gentile breakthrough in Antioch that led to the famous Jerusalem Council recorded in Acts 15*. As long as the number of Gentiles remained small, then the Jews had various ways of accommodating Gentiles within a larger Jewish movement that retained Jewish identity. However, the growth of the Gentile movement forced the Jerusalem Council to meet in AD 49. The decision of the Council of Jerusalem was in favor of *one* body of Christ, but *multiple* cultures within the broad parameters of Christian morality. In short, the church embraced the idea of a diverse church, opening the door to a potentially infinite number of cultural expressions that could all be authentically Christian. Excepting any ethnic Jews who are following Christ and reading this book, every Christian who is reading these pages is indebted to these earliest unnamed Christians who crossed that first cultural boundary with the good news of Jesus. We are Christians because someone followed in their footsteps and preached the gospel to our ancestors. In short, this picture is our story, and it all began with these two disciples from Cyprus and Cyrene, who boldly decided to tell Gentiles "the good news about the Lord Jesus."

CHAPTER 2

St. Thomas Preaches the Gospel in India

My second snapshot is a picture of St. Thomas, commonly known in the church as "Doubting Thomas." Let me tell you the rest of the story. All of the Gospels record a final, Great Commission of Jesus to His disciples. In John's gospel he records those powerful words of Jesus to His disciples, "As the Father has sent me, I am sending you" (John 20:21). However, John records that Thomas was not with them that evening (20:24). When Thomas heard about the appearance, he famously declared that unless he saw the nail-scarred hands of Jesus and put his finger into them and into His sword-pierced side, he would not believe (20:25). Because of this declaration, Thomas has become known as Doubting Thomas. It seems that the church has sometimes forgotten that one week later, when Thomas himself saw the risen Lord, he made the most powerful declaration of the deity of Christ found in any of the Gospels: "My Lord and my God!" (20:28).

Although there are important traditions surrounding the ministries of all the apostles, we will focus our second high-light on the St. Thomas mission to India, which is one of the oldest and strongest traditions in church history. The earliest record of the mission of Thomas to India is found in an early manuscript known as the *Acts of Thomas,* which dates around the turn of the third century. This manuscript records a dramatic moment where the eleven apostles all gathered in Jerusalem and divided the known world into various regions.

They then cast lots to determine where each of them would go. India fell to Thomas. According to the account, Thomas objected, saying that because of his "weakness of the flesh" he could not travel. However, Christ appeared to him in a vision and promised to be with him. Thomas eventually traveled by ship to India along one of the well-established trade routes to India, arriving in AD 52. He preached the gospel in various locations in India and finally suffered martyrdom in India and was buried near modern-day Chennai.

Although the *Acts of Thomas* has problems, many historians accept the basic historical nucleus of the account. The Western tradition has a number of corroborating references, and there is also archaeological evidence from India, as well as an independent Indian tradition that chronicles precise numbers of people healed from various diseases and maladies and detailed accounts of those who were converted, including what caste they were from. These sources also give a rich description of the circumstances around the martyrdom of Thomas.

The specific details of these traditional accounts are not nearly as important as the core historical claim that, even if we cannot speak with certainty regarding any of the details, St. Thomas brought the gospel to India in the first century. This vignette from mission history is important for our study for three reasons. First, *the Thomas tradition highlights the multi-directional mission of the early church.* This tradition represents the oldest documented account of the church in Asia beyond the borders of the Roman Empire. Paul's missionary journeys, as recorded in Acts, detail the movement of the gospel further into the West. There is no parallel account to the book of Acts that tells the story of the gospel's advance into the East. Therefore, very few Christians who read the book of Acts realize that at about the same time that Acts 19 records the apostle Paul preaching in Ephesus, the apostle Thomas is preaching the gospel in India. The book of Acts is not intended to give us a comprehensive picture of the entire early Gentile mission, but rather highlights the spread of the gospel to the seat of the

Roman Empire. It is important for you to realize that, from the beginning, the spread of the gospel was multidirectional.

Second, the tradition of Thomas also underscores the importance of *recognizing the multiple layers of Christian tradition that are often present in Asian Christianity*. The apostolic tradition of Thomas is but the first of a series of initiatives into India. The apostolic tradition of Thomas is followed by the arrival of Syriac Christians bringing an Eastern liturgy in the fourth century. This is followed years later by major Roman Catholic initiatives beginning with the arrival of Francis Xavier in 1542. Later, India receives Protestant missionaries with the arrival of the Lutheran missionaries Ziegenbalg and Plütschau in 1706. These are all examples of distinct traditions, all of which coexist in India until the present day. Diverse expressions of Christianity arrived at different times in different parts of India, and they all interacted in various ways, not only with the Hindu traditions, but also with the various Christian traditions as well.

Third, the presence of Christianity in ancient India also highlights the *difficulties in speaking without qualification of Hinduism as the "indigenous" religion of India.* Some accounts of Christianity in India leave the impression that Christianity in India is a movement that coincides with the British colonial presence in India. It should be remembered, however, that the early religious forms of what is today known as Hinduism came from migrating Aryans who originated outside of India. There are many people groups in India who were Christians for centuries before the British presence in India.

In conclusion, the Thomas tradition reminds us that although the apostle Thomas may have come to believe in the resurrection of Jesus Christ a week after the other apostles, he went on to become one of the greatest cross-cultural missionaries of the first century. We should not keep calling him Doubting Thomas. Instead, we should call him "Believing Thomas" because he not only gives us the most explicit declaration of the deity of Christ in the Gospels ("My

Lord, and my God!"), but he ends up bringing the gospel farther than any of the other apostles and even gave his life as an early Christian martyr. What a great story! If you have had a difficult chapter in your life, as Thomas did, don't stop believing that God still has a wonderful plan for your life!

CHAPTER 3

The Tale of Two Monks: Alopen and Augustine

The third picture is of two monks who lived during the seventh century, in two completely different parts of the world. The first story is associated with the papacy of Pope Gregory the Great. Gregory is hailed by Roman Catholic Christians as one of the great missionary popes. According to the Benedictine historian Venerable Bede (672–735), Gregory encountered several young, blond-haired, blue-eyed boys being sold in the slave market. He inquired as to their ethnic origin and, upon hearing that they were Angles, he famously replied, *"Non Angli, sed Angeli,"* i.e., they are not Angles, but Angels. This led to his dispatching St. Augustine of Canterbury on a mission to the Anglo-Saxon kingdoms in 596. Despite significant reluctance, Augustine, along with forty monks, arrived in 597 and was warmly received by King Ethelbert of Kent, who was married to a Christian princess named Bertha from Gaul. Over the next year not only was the king baptized, but approximately ten thousand Saxons were baptized. However, Augustine became deeply concerned not only about the superficial nature of their conversion, but also about a wide range of customs that these new believers were bringing into the church. The reply of Pope Gregory the Great in AD 601 has become one of the classic mission letters in history.

The most important part of the letter reads as follows:

The heathen temples of these people need not be destroyed, only the idols which are to be found in them. . . . If the temples are well built, it is a good idea to detach them from the service of the devil, and to adapt them for the worship of the true God. . . . And since the people are accustomed, when they assemble for sacrifice, to kill many oxen in sacrifice to the devils, it seems reasonable to appoint a festival for the people by way of exchange. The people must learn to slay their cattle not in honor of the devil, but in honor of God and for their own food; when they have eaten and are full, then they must render thanks to the giver of all good things. If we allow them these outward joys, they are more likely to find their way to the true inner joy. . . . It is doubtless impossible to cut off all abuses at once from rough hearts, just as the man who sets out to climb a high mountain does not advance by leaps and bounds, but goes upward step by step and pace by pace.[1]

This letter gives us a remarkable insight into a very early period of Christian missions. It demonstrates how various cultural challenges and the pastoral needs of new believers are as old as the gospel itself.

However, before we reflect further on this early-seventh-century letter, we need to travel from England in the West to China in the East. In 1623, some workmen digging near the city of Xian—the ancient capital of the T'ang dynasty—uncovered a massive limestone monument more than nine feet high. At the top of the monument was carved a cross rising out of a lotus blossom. The inscription beneath tells the story of the Nestorian mission to China headed up by a monk named Alopen in AD 635. The following is a selection from the inscription on the Nestorian monument:

> Fulfilling the old law as it was declared by the twenty-four Sages, He (the Messiah) taught how to rule both families and kingdoms according to His own great Plan. Establishing His New Teaching of Nonassertion which operates silently through the Holy Spirit, another Person of the Trinity, He formed in humanity the capacity for well-doing through the Right Faith. Setting up the standard of the eight cardinal virtues, He purged away the dust from human nature and perfected a true character. . . . He brought Life to Light and abolished Death. . . . He swept away the abodes of darkness. All the evil devices of the devil were thereupon defeated and destroyed. He then took an oar in the Vessel of Mercy and ascended to the Palace of Light. . . . The Great Means of Conversion (or leavening, i.e., transformation) were

widely extended, and the sealed Gate of the Blessed Life was
unlocked. . . . His law is to bathe with water and the Spirit,
and thus to cleanse from all vain Delusions. . . . (His ministers) carry the Cross with them as a Sign. They travel about
wherever the sun shines and try to reunite those that are
beyond the pale (i.e., those that are lost).[2]

It is fascinating that the arrival of Augustine of Canterbury
to the Saxons and the arrival of Alopen to the Chinese court
occur fewer than forty years apart. Our general familiarity
with the Western missionary expansion often eclipses the
remarkable expansion of the gospel along the silk route by
Nestorian missionaries.

There are two important lessons to be drawn from the
work of these two bands of monks, led by Augustine and
Alopen. *First, we should observe the deep commitment of these early
missionaries to communicate the gospel into new cultural settings.*
The letter from Gregory the Great and the monument to
the Nestorian mission both demonstrate deep reflection
concerning how to best communicate the gospel. Gregory

the Great's letter established three principles, which continue to guide missionaries today.

First, he established the principle of *adaptation* in relation to cultural forms. He told Augustine not to destroy the well-built temples, but simply to cleanse them of the idols that are to be found within. The pagan temples were thereby able to be adopted and used as places of Christian worship. Second, he established the principle of *exchange* in relation to pagan practices. Gregory the Great wisely understood that it is not sufficient to simply condemn the pagan sacrifices that played such a central role in the religious life of the Saxons. He instructed Augustine to tell the new believers to give up their pagan sacrifices, but to provide an alternative Christian ritual that allowed them to sacrifice their animals in praise to God. Christians may disagree about whether this was good advice, but it is important to recognize the principle that is involved and which countless missionaries have faced over the centuries. Finally, Gregory set forth the principle of *gradual transformation*. He realized that the Saxon community would not be transformed overnight, and so he encouraged Augustine to allow time for the Holy Spirit to work in the lives of the new believers. It would be several generations before the Saxons were discipled into full-orbed faith and practice.

The Nestorian monument demonstrates that the Nestorians did not impose a Western gospel on the Chinese and insist that it be stated in precisely the same way they had learned the gospel. The T'ang dynasty was a period when Confucianism and Buddhism were both thriving. The Nestorian missionaries related the truths of the gospel in a way that drew heavily from the current religious under-standing of the Chinese. Yet, despite the use of language and terms that sound strange to Western ears, one cannot help but discern in reading the entire inscription that the Nestorian monks were equally committed to communi-cating the Christian gospel.

Second, as noted with the apostle Thomas's mission to India, *we should recognize the antiquity of Christianity in Asia.* Later, Roman Catholic and Protestant missionaries arrived in China and discovered that the message of the gospel had *already preceded them*. This is an important reminder that this is God's story and that we are just participants in His work. Missionaries have sometimes mistakenly seen their role as "bringing the gospel" to a particular people group. However, one of the important lessons is to recognize God's primary agency in the missionary task. The missionaries did not bring the gospel to China; God brought the missionaries to China. After the dramatic conversion of the Saxons, Augustine inquired about a suitable location to build a church. To the surprise of Augustine, Queen Bertha brought him to a site of the ruins of an even earlier Christian church that had been constructed centuries before. It is thought that the gospel's first entrance into England probably came through unnamed soldiers of the Roman Empire who had been converted. The gospel spreads not just through the officially commissioned missionaries, but also through countless ordinary believers who, wherever they go, bear witness to the good news of Jesus Christ.

CHAPTER 4

Raymond Lull and the Challenge of Islam

Our fourth picture is a robust-looking man named Raymond Lull. But let me begin by explaining something of the background that brought this man into the life of the church.

It is difficult for us to fully imagine how the rapid spread of Islam beginning in the seventh century affected the psyche of the average Christian in the Middle Ages. Muhammad died in AD 632. Within four years Islamic

armies had captured Damascus and Antioch. By 638 they
had laid siege to Jerusalem and captured it in only four
months, followed soon by the fall of Caesarea (640) and
Alexandria (642). Islamic armies eventually crossed over into
Europe and captured most of Spain and would have pene-
trated even deeper into Europe if they had not been stopped
by Charles Martel at the Battle of Tours in AD 732. However,
Islam continued to spread into North and East Africa and
deep into Asia. Within a few centuries, the Islamic Empire
stretched from Spain in the West, across North Africa, the
Middle East, and portions of central Asia. Although the
Byzantine Empire did not officially fall until 1453 when the
Muslims sacked Constantinople, the threat of Islam was an
ongoing source of anxiety and speculation throughout the
entire Middle Ages.

The Christian response to the rise of Islam is mostly
remembered as a series of military campaigns launched by
Western Christendom against Islam known as the Crusades.
The seven campaigns, or Crusades, took place between 1095

and 1250. The reasons for the Crusades were complex and intertwined, ranging from a desire to safeguard pilgrims to the Holy Land, to the search for new sources of wealth, to the need to strengthen the waning power of the papacy. However, the central long-term objective was to defeat the Islamic armies and to retake the Holy Land, thus reclaiming lost territories for Christendom. From both a military and a spiritual perspective, the Crusades were a total failure. Indeed, the memory of the Crusades continues to inform Islamic attitudes about Christianity even to the present day.

It is important to realize, however, that the Crusades are not the *only* story of the Christian response to Islam during the Middle Ages. The fourth historical focus highlights the life and ministry of Raymond Lull (1232–1315), known as the "Father of Islamic Apologetics." Lull was born at one of the most remarkable and tumultuous times in history. During his lifetime, Spain was being liberated from Islamic domination. Within the first few decades of his life, he would live to see the rise of the Ottoman Turks, the dismal failure of the seventh crusade, and the founding of the first college of Oxford University.

Lull, by his own account, was a licentious young man and, even after marriage, engaged in several adulterous relationships. He was a well-known poet and skilled musician in the Christian court of Aragon, where he grew up. However, after a dramatic vision of Christ, Lull was powerfully converted in his early thirties and became a dedicated follower of Christ. He was deeply disturbed by the hateful and militaristic attitude of Christians toward Muslims that was prevalent in his day. He was dismayed to realize that no Christian writer was responding to the philosophical challenges that had been posed by the famous Islamic philosophers of his time. Lull decided to dedicate his life to finding a way to effectively communicate the gospel to Muslims.

With nearly three hundred published works, Lull's writings are vast, covering political theory, poetry, mathematics, science, philosophy, and theology. Early on in his writings, Lull recognized the need to develop a Christian apologetic that specifically and directly responded to Islamic misunderstandings and objections to Christianity. Lull spent nine years learning Arabic and carefully studying Islamic philosophy and theology. Eventually he developed a multivolume, Trinitarian apologetic, known as *Ars Generalis ultima* (the Ultimate General Art), which answered Islamic objections to Christianity and advocated a method for talking to Muslims, sometimes known as the Lullian method. Lull was convinced that the military confrontation represented by the Crusades was a mistake. Rather, he believed that Muslims should be addressed in love, not hate, and by the force of logic, not the instruments of war.

Lull also recognized the need to train and mobilize an entire new movement of monks who would go into the Muslim world as missionaries. Lull called on the pope and the princes of Christendom to establish monasteries for the study of Arabic and other languages spoken by Islamic peoples in order to train them in his "method" and send them out to turn the Islamic world to Christ. Lull wrote:

I see many knights going to the Holy Land in the expectation of conquering it by force or arms; but instead of accomplishing this object, they are in the end all swept away themselves. Therefore, it is my belief that the conquest of the Holy Land should be attempted in no other way than as Christ and his apostles undertook to accomplish it; by love, by prayer, by tears, and by the offering up of our own lives. It seems that the possession of the Holy Sepulchre can be better secured by the force of preaching than by the force of arms, therefore let monks march forth as holy knights . . . and proclaim to the infidels the truth of his passion.[1]

Lull eventually secured the support for this plan from Pope John XXI.

Lull insisted that everyone trained in his method be willing to suffer for the sake of the gospel. Given the ongoing conflicts with Islam in his day, this was a sober realization by Lull of the inherent dangers in any Islamic mission. Lull made at least four missionary journeys to Islamic North Africa. He was able to present his apologetic defense of Christianity to Muslim leaders. However, he also suffered expulsions, abuse, and long imprisonments. Finally, when he was in his eighties, he preached to a gathering of Muslims in Algiers and was stoned to death.

Lull was really ahead of his time, recognizing the ill effects of military responses to Islam and the positive benefits of answering questions that they have. He also understood that if we are to make headway with Muslims, we must be willing to suffer. Lull's ministry and scholarship have given him many titles, including *Doctor Illuminatus*, father of Islamic apologetics and father of Islamic missions. However, perhaps his most important and enduring title is the Apostle of Love in an age of hate.

CHAPTER 5

From Padroado (1493) to Propaganda Fide (1622)

This fifth historical snapshot is not focused on one particular individual, but on a very influential period in the history of Roman Catholic missions. When Columbus returned to Spain from his famous voyage to the New World, his ship was blown off course and he landed in Lisbon, Portugal. King John II saw this as an opportunity to claim that all the territorial discoveries made by Columbus belonged to Portugal.

Searching for a western route to Asia was considered vital to bypassing Islamic powers that controlled the traditional routes to the East. King Ferdinand and Queen Isabella of Spain sent ambassadors to Rome to resolve the conflict. On May 4, 1493, Pope Alexander VI issued a papal bull that created a line of demarcation that ran longitudinally "one hundred leagues towards the west and south" from the Azores and Cape Verde Islands. This line down the Atlantic, known as the Padroado, essentially granted special patronage to Spain in the West and to Portugal to the East. A year later, the line was moved 370 degrees west, granting Portugal a foothold in the New World, allowing them to colonize Brazil, which explains why Portuguese is spoken in Brazil.

The Padroado raises important questions about the relationship of Christian missions and colonization. It is commonly believed that missions were but the vanguard of colonial imperialism and colonialism, in turn, operated under the guise of divine sanction. Today, churches often carry a strong sense of guilt about the whole missionary enterprise, largely because missions has become associated with the colonial movement and imperialism toward weaker countries. It is important to remember, however, that the missionary movement and the colonial movement coincided in time, but were two distinct movements. There are, of course, examples of embarrassing entanglements whereby missionaries were co-opted by the secular authorities. However, we should resist the temptation to see missions and colonialism as two sides of one coin. In fact, I have chosen two missionaries during this period to highlight how distinct the movements really were.

The first picture we want to look at is Bartolomé de las Casas (1484–1566), who immigrated to the island of Hispaniola in the Caribbean in 1502. Upon his arrival he was shocked by the cruel treatment of the Indians by the colonial authorities. He eventually was ordained as a Dominican priest and became a fierce critic of Spanish colonial practices. The governor of Hispaniola gave Spanish settlers Indians as slaves, ostensibly in return for Christian instruction. Las Casas carefully documented the atrocities of the conquistadors and was instrumental in not only getting laws passed to protect the rights of indigenous peoples, but in stimulating an important theological debate about Christian attitudes toward human rights. Las Casas articulated a doctrine of natural human rights that was well ahead of his time, earning him the title "Protector of the Indians" in 1516.

Another picture we should look at is that of Alessandro Valignano, who was born into an Italian noble family and joined the Society of Jesus (Jesuits) in 1566. In 1573 he was appointed director of all the Jesuit work in the East, and he is considered the architect of the Jesuit mission to Asia. He made regular trips to India, China, and Japan. He wrote policies and established a number of important principles that continue to inform missionary work today. Some examples are as follows. *First, he distinguished between European culture and the essentials of the Christian faith. Second, because of tensions with Spain and Portugal during the post-Padroado period, he pointed out the inevitable problems when the state is given sovereignty over missionary work. He argued for a necessary independence from Portugal in the missionary work in Asia. Third, he rejected the conquistador principle, which had undergirded the Crusades and supported the notion of using military action to gain former Christian lands that had been seized by Muslims. Fourth, he encouraged his missionaries, wherever possible, to affirm Japanese cultural practices, and even encouraged the ordination of Japanese priests.*

These two men set into motion many dramatic changes in the relationship of the church to the state. Furthermore, they showed a sensitivity to culture and to human rights that has been a hallmark of Christian faith.

CHAPTER 6

Count Nicolaus von Zinzendorf and the Moravian Mission

Popular missionary literature often cites William Carey as the father of the modern Protestant missionary movement. However, the actual story of Protestant missions begins long before William Carey. In fact, many people do not even know that an entire Protestant missionary movement occurred *before* William Carey. So, I have decided to tell you a little bit about the life of Count Nicolaus Von Zinzendorf, who sparked the Moravian missionary movement.

The Moravian missionary movement arose out of a seventeenth- and eighteenth-century movement known as Pietism. Pietism was a renewal movement that emphasized personal devotion, Bible study, sermons, and the role of the laity. Many of the key themes of Pietism are found in Philip Jacob Spener's classic work *Pia Desideria* (Pious Desires), published in 1675. The full scope and far-ranging influences of Pietism on Christianity are too many to recount here. However, it is important for you to know that the sixteenth-century Protestant Reformation did not produce any missionaries. It was the advent of Pietism two centuries later that produced the first Protestant missionaries, Bartholomäus Ziegenbalg and Henry Plütschau, who went to India in 1705 through the Danish-Halle mission. However, the Moravians and the mobilization efforts of Count Nicolaus von Zinzendorf will be the focus of this historical spotlight because the Moravians represent the first major Protestant missionary *movement*.

Count Nicolaus von Zinzendorf (1700–1760) grew up under the influence of Pietism. Much of his early years were spent in Halle, Germany, under the influence of Auguste Francke, one of the great figures of early Pietism. In 1722, Zinzendorf, a wealthy German nobleman, purchased a large estate in Berthelsdorf (eastern Germany), which he allowed to be used as a refuge for Christians from Bohemia and Moravia (present-day Czech Republic) who were fleeing persecution from the established church.

Although the Moravian church did not become a separate denomination until the 1740s, it has roots in the fourteenth-century Hussite movement associated with the dissenter John Hus. Often cited as a pre-Reformation Protestant, John Hus was one of the earliest critics of abuses that were present in Roman Catholicism at that time. Hus's followers eventually formed a movement known as the Unity of the Brethren

(*Unitas Fratrum*), which continued as an early "Protestant" movement. However, the movement was often persecuted and existed primarily as an underground movement. In 1722 the Brethren took refuge at Zinzendorf's estate. The number of refugees eventually grew to more than three hundred, including some dissenting German Pietists who also joined the Brethren. They named the place where this community formed Herrnhut, meaning, "The Lord's Watch."

On August 13, 1727, the community received a powerful outpouring of the Holy Spirit, causing a dramatic revival among the Brethren. Many who were there described it as a Pentecost-like event that brought a powerful sense of unity, prayerfulness, spiritual fervor, and renewed dedication to Jesus Christ. Under the guidance, itinerancy, and mobilization of Zinzendorf—who in 1737 was consecrated as the bishop of the church—the *Unitas Fratum*, now known as the Moravians, become a major force for world evangelization. They eventually sent hundreds of missionaries all over the world, including the Caribbean, North and South America, the Arctic, Africa, the Middle East, and India.

There are several vital lessons that we can learn from this first Protestant missionary movement. First, *the Moravians were deeply committed to pray for the evangelization of the world.* The dramatic move of God in their midst on August 13, 1727, was so profound that they continued taking turns in maintaining a prayer vigil. The Moravians focused their "Prayer Wall" on the evangelization of the world. This prayer vigil was maintained twenty-four hours a day, seven days a week for more than one hundred years! The entire "great century" of Protestant missions is birthed out of the fervent prayers of the Moravians at Herrnhut!

Second, the Moravians were the first modern group of Christians to fully recognize that *the missionary enterprise was the primary work of all Christians,* not just a few selected specialists. Because of their history of persecution and displacement as refugees, the Moravians were accustomed to adversity and travel. Therefore, they made excellent missionaries. They mobilized the laity in big numbers and refused to accept the idea that ministry should only be done by ordained clergy.

Third, *the Moravians were self-supporting missionaries*. The Moravians understood that a professionalized missionary force would require extensive financial and logistical support to maintain. To support full-time professional missionaries would require up to 90 percent of the church to remain home in order to generate sufficient disposable income to support the missionaries. Instead, the Moravians opted for a lay mission force that would be completely self-supporting through the practice of their own trade.

The first Moravian missionary to be sent out from Herrnhut is representative of many who followed. Leonhard Dober (1706–1766) had traveled 315 miles on foot to get to Herrnhut, arriving in 1725. He was, by trade, a potter, as his father had been before him. While at Herrnhut he experienced the spiritual awakening that took place in 1727. Like many of the Brethren, he loved music and served the community by directing the choir and composing hymns, revealing the ongoing influence of Pietism in the community. Later, Zinzendorf introduced to the community a former African slave known as Anton, who had become a Christian. The slave challenged the community to send missionaries to work with African slaves. After a sleepless night in prayer, Dober committed himself to become a missionary to African slaves. On August 21, 1732, Dober was sent from Herrnhut to the malaria-infested island of St. Thomas in the Caribbean, where he ministered to African slaves. He was sent out (along with a carpenter named David Nitschmann) and charged to support himself by his own hands. Dober went on to have a long and distinguished career as a missionary, general elder, and later, bishop of the Moravian church.

Finally, the Moravians were known *to send missionaries to difficult places to work among marginalized peoples*. The work among slaves on St. Thomas is, once again, representative of the Moravian commitment to the margins of society. Precisely because the Moravians were themselves a marginalized and persecuted community, they had a special burden for other displaced and suffering peoples. This commitment often came at great sacrifice. For example, of the eighteen missionaries who were eventually sent from Herrnhut to work with the slaves on St. Thomas, half died within the first six months.

While the Moravian church has never been large, it has exerted an influence well beyond its size. Influential Christian leaders such as John Wesley and William Carey have all paid tribute to the formative role the Moravians played in their spiritual formation.

CHAPTER 7

The Odd Origins of Korean Christianity

Despite being one of the last countries in Asia to receive the Christian message, Korea has one of the most fascinating and unusual origins of any church in the world. The history of "the Hermit Kingdom" has been marked by numerous invasions and periods of isolation from outside contact. One of the most important invasions of Korea took place in 1592 when the Japanese army of Toyotomi Hideyoshi sent nine army divisions to crush Korea. Many Koreans were taken back to Japanese prison camps, where they met Jesuit priests who, at that time, were permitted to work in Japan.

One of the Jesuit missionaries who worked in these Japanese prison camps was named Father Fróis (1532–1597). He reported that there were at least three hundred Koreans being held by the Japanese in Nagasaki alone. Interestingly, there were no known Christians in Korea at this time, but Koreans were becoming Christians in Japanese prison camps. In fact, the presence of Korean Christians in Japanese prison camps was confirmed during the persecution following the 1614 Edict. Japanese records indicate hundreds of Korean prisoners who were put to death for their faith along with the Japanese. Because Korea was closed to outside missionaries, it became necessary to work with expatriate Koreans who were being held in Japan. It is ironic that Koreans were already being martyred for their faith even before there were any known Christians in Korea.

Other influences came to Korea via China. Around 1770 the Korean ambassador to China, Chong tu-won, brought back to Korea Matteo Ricci's *Tianzhu,* or *True Doctrine of the Lord of Heaven*. This and other works gradually trickled in from China during these years. One young Korean scholar, known as Yi Pyok, was a part of an intellectual movement known as the Shilhak School (School of Practical Learning). They were interested in learning from the Western world and were open to studying thinking from outside of Korea. In 1783 these Shilkak scholars asked Yi Sang-Hung (Lee Seung-Hun), the son of the ambassador, if while he was at the imperial court he could also visit the Catholic missionaries in China and learn all that he could about Christianity. The twenty-seven-year-old Yi was instructed by the Jesuits and was baptized in Beijing before his return to Korea. When Yi returned to Korea in 1784, now with the baptismal name Peter Lee Seung-Hun, he brought with him Christian literature from China, which he distributed to the Shilhak scholars. They decided that Christianity would be beneficial to Korea because it established authority based on merit, not based on birth, and because the basic ethics of Christianity were not in major conflict with Confucian ethics. Peter Lee baptized a Korean believer, Lee Pyok, renamed him "John-Baptist," and they started to baptize others and ordain priests. This marks the beginning of Christian missionaries being permitted to spread the gospel in Korea.

There are three important observations about the emergence of Korean Christianity that are crucial to our understanding of the emergence of global Christianity. First, *Korea is one of the few countries in the world where the church was born outside of the country through expatriates who were being held as prisoners.* Second, *the first missionaries to Korea were not foreign missionaries, but the Koreans themselves who had come to Christ outside of Korea and returned as indigenous propagators of the gospel.* Third, *one of the earliest documentations of the Christian message was from Chinese Christian documents, rather than literature that explained the gospel in Western terminology.* Since Korea has become one of the most Christianized countries in Asia and today is the home of the largest Christian churches in the world, it is important to recall the unusual origins of Korean Christianity, which was brought to birth through indigenous expressions of faith. If you want proof that God's Unfolding Story is about God's initiative, after which He uses us to work with Him, then the Korean church represents one of the foremost examples.

Act Two

The Great Century
of Missions,
1792–1910

Introduction

The ancient Greeks had two different words for time. The first word, *chronos*, is where we get our word *chronology* from. It refers to ordinary "clock time," which is measured in history and is marked when someone says, for example, the Battle of Hastings took place in 1066. The other word for time is *kairos*, which has a more qualitative, not merely quantitative, dimension to it. It refers to a specially appointed time, an opportune moment, or the right timing. Jesus, for example, calls us to recognize the "signs of the *times*" (Matt. 16:3, italics mine). When He announces the in-breaking of the kingdom of God, He says, "The *time* has come. The kingdom of God is at hand" (Mark 1:15). In both of these examples, Jesus uses the word *kairos*, indicating that He is not merely referring to a point of chronology, but a decisive moment in the history of God's purposes in the world.

This distinction between *chronos* and *kairos* is important as we continue in these historical reflections. In act 1 we discovered that mission history is about much more than just being able to chronologically tabulate all the things that have happened in history. Instead, we sought to highlight seven key moments in early missions history in order to gain some perspective as we move into the modern period.

Act 2 will focus on the remarkable period between 1792 and 1910, which, in my view, represents one of these *kairos* periods in the history of the church. The period spans from the publication of *An Enquiry* by William Carey to the 1910 conference in Edinburgh, which is regarded as the world's first global missionary conference. During that period, which is roughly coterminous with the nineteenth century, more new Christians emerged from a wider number of new people groups than at any previous time in the history of the church. Never before had so many Christians moved to so many vast and remote parts of the globe and communicated the gospel across so many cultural boundaries. Looking back from this perspective, we can see even more clearly what an amazing time it was for the Western church. The twentieth century would witness the surprising and dramatic decline of the Western church and the equally surprising and dramatic rise of the church in the Majority World. The seeds planted in the nineteenth century are bearing remarkable fruit in the twenty-first century. Who would have believed that in such a short time, the English-speaking world, which for a period was the center of global missionary sending, would now be *receiving missionaries* from the new vibrant centers of African, Asian, and Latin American Christianity! It is thrilling to see those who received the gospel, now bringing the gospel back to the West and reminding the West of that which has been largely forgotten.

As with act 1, the purpose of act 2 is not to convey a vast, detailed account of this remarkable period, which the imminent church historian Kenneth Scott Latourette called the "Great Century." Rather, our purpose is to highlight some key themes or trends that can help establish a framework for seeing the big picture that unfolded during this remarkable *kairos* moment in the history of world Christianity. Rather than focusing on key people, as in act 1, this part of the book will focus on five defining themes that give shape and force to the Great Century.

CHAPTER 8

Holy Subversion: The Birth of the Protestant Missionary Society

One of the curiosities in the history of missions is why William Carey became known as the "Father of Modern Missions." He was not the first modern missionary, the first Protestant missionary, or even the first Baptist missionary. We have already examined the remarkable Moravian missionary movement, which preceded Carey by six decades and sent missionaries all over the world, including India.

This first defining theme of act 2 helps explain why William Carey *can* be referred to as the Father of Modern Missions. William Carey is the Father of Modern Missions not just because of what he accomplished in India, but primarily because he stimulated the founding of dozens of new voluntary missionary *societies*, propelling hundreds of new missionaries out onto the field in what became the largest-scale missions mobilization in history. Some of you may have never even heard of William Carey, so we will begin by looking at his life, and then we can more fully appreciate his role in starting the voluntary mission society that has so changed the history of missions.

William Carey was born in England on August 17, 1761. There is little in his early life that would have given any indication of the dramatic way God would use Carey. He was from a very poor family from a tiny village. He had a skin disease that prevented long exposure to the sun, so he became a cobbler. He belonged to the Particular Baptists, widely despised at the time for being religious nonconformists. In every way—economically, socially, and religiously—Carey represented someone at the margins of his society. However, in the providence of God, Carey had become a Christian and had become ordained as a pastor of a small Baptist church. We first get a glimpse into the zeal of Carey when he challenged his fellow ministers to dedicate one of their monthly meetings to the question, Does the commission given by our Lord Jesus Christ to His disciples still apply to us today? This discussion eventually led Carey to write and publish in 1792 an eighty-seven-page book, which has been called the most influential missionary tract ever written in English. A close examination of the title of the book is very important. Carey called his book *An Enquiry into the Obligation of Christians to Use Means for the Conversion of the Heathens*. It was not unusual at that time for books to have long, descriptive titles rather than the shorter, often more obscure titles that are given to books today.

The title of Carey's treatise falls into three major parts. The first part, *An Enquiry into the Obligation of Christians*, reveals the historical and theological obstacles that Carey faced in becoming a missionary. The latter part of the title, *for the Conversion of the Heathens*, reveals Carey's firm commitment to the gospel of Jesus Christ and the need for all peoples to hear and to respond to the gospel. It is the *middle* of the three parts of the book's title that has been the most neglected, and yet is arguably the most important. It is the phrase *to use means*. In this tiny phrase lay the remarkable genius of William Carey and, fascinatingly, the reason why he is known today as the Father of Modern Missions.

The phrase *to use means* points to the responsibility of Christians to organize themselves and form some structure that would allow them to support missionaries around the world. The Roman Catholics have a long history of allowing a wide range of alliances, known as mission societies, which could focus on and address specific needs, including youth ministry, missions, charitable work, and so forth. Today, many people admire and are acquainted with the late Mother Teresa's Missionaries of Charity, a society dedicated to serving the poorest of the poor and now operates in more than one hundred different countries. During the Protestant Reformation, the Reformers did not carry over the idea of creating these societies in the church. Therefore, one of the main reasons why Protestants did not send any missionaries out for the first two hundred years was not only *theological*; it was also profoundly *structural*. Although Carey's *Enquiry* is filled with solid theology and history, this is not the source of the radical nature of Carey's proposal. Carey, as a Protestant, had no ecclesiastical structures to look to for guidance. So, he proposed a mission society based largely upon the model of secular trading societies that were being organized for commercial purposes. Carey wrote:

> Suppose a company of serious Christians, ministers and private persons, were to form themselves into a society, and make a number of rules respecting the regulation of the plan, and the persons who are to be employed as missionaries, the means of defraying the expense, etc., etc.[1]

Here was a very secular structure—quite un-theological on the surface—which was, in fact, one of the most important theological developments in Protestantism. However, gradually these lay associations not only generated recruits to become missionaries, but eventually generated considerable amounts of money to provide for their support. A new kind of structure was emerging among Protestant churches, which was, inadvertently creating a new power base. The mission society represented a kind of "holy subversion" of a recalcitrant church. The implications this had for lay ministry, for enabling women to exercise their gifts cross-culturally, and for achieving specific, Christian goals in faraway places was enormous.

Within a few short years of Carey's proposal to create a mission society, more than a dozen new mission societies began to spring up on both sides of the Atlantic. The birth of the mission society had created a new structure that would enable thousands of people to relocate cross-culturally for full-time mission service. The Baptist Missionary Society, the

London Missionary Society, the Church Missionary Society, the Religious Tract Society, the British and Foreign Bible Society, the American Board of Commissioners for Foreign Missions, and the American Baptist Missionary Board are just a few of the early societies that helped to launch this remarkably vibrant period of Protestant missions.

Today, when a student walks into my office and tells me that they are interested in becoming a missionary, I have at my fingertips a catalog of all the mission agencies in North America, many of which have very specific and focused ministries. The catalog is more than six hundred pages long, listing hundreds of mission organizations. The mission societies collectively made the Great Century possible and continue to be the greatest resource for missions mobilization in the world. Carey's call to "use means" was, looking back, a spark that ignited one of the great movements in the history of the church, the birth of the Protestant missionary society.

CHAPTER 9

The Word Made Text: Vernacular Bible Translations

Christianity is the only world religion whose primary source documents are in a language other than the language of the founder of the religion. This is unheard-of among world religions. Muhammad spoke Arabic and the Qur'an is in Arabic; the Brahmin priests in India spoke Sanskrit and the Upanishads are in Sanskrit. Jesus spoke Aramaic, and yet the primary documents that record Christ's teachings are not in Aramaic, but in Koine Greek, the language of Gentile Hellenism. This is a remarkable testimony to the glorious truth that the gospel of Jesus Christ can be placed in any language in the world!

Christians affirm that the gospel retains its power even as it is made intelligible and announced in specific, local contexts in myriad new languages. This means that the gospel could be expressed with new language forms, while retaining its transforming power. Thus, translating the Bible into a vernacular language is an important theological assertion about the translatability of the Christian gospel. This is in contrast with, for example, the Muslims, who maintain the Qur'an is untranslatable and the word of Allah can only be conveyed in Arabic. Likewise, Hindu priests have traditionally taught that the mantras of ancient Hinduism lose their power when they are uttered in a vernacular language.

Tragically, the theological importance of the translatability of the Word of God has not always been recognized by the church. The church resisted vernacular translations, and eventually the attitude developed that the only three languages into which the Bible could be translated were the three languages of the inscription placed on the cross of Christ (Aramaic, Greek, and Latin; see John 19:20). With the plethora of various translations available today, it is difficult for some Christians to imagine how William Tyndale (1494–1536), who was the first to complete a full translation of the Bible into English, had to do so in secret, smuggling the Bibles into England and Scotland from Germany. When Tyndale's New Testament was published, Cardinal Wolsey condemned the work and called for Tyndale's arrest. He was eventually arrested, imprisoned, tried for heresy, and burned at the stake for his effort.

One of the most important victories of the Reformation was reestablishing the principle of the linguistic translatability of the Bible. Martin Luther's translation of the Bible into German (1522–1534) was not only a major literary landmark in the history of the German language, but a vital theological statement on behalf of the whole church. It set the stage for what would, in time, become a dramatic rise in vernacular Bible translations by Protestant missionaries.

The commitment to Bible translation is one of the major hallmarks of the Great Century of missions. A few examples will help to illustrate the trend. Robert Morrison (1782–1834) arrived in China (Canton) in 1807. By 1823 the entire Bible was published in Chinese. Adoniram Judson (1788–1850), the famous American pioneer missionary, went to Burma in 1812 and translated the entire Bible into Burmese by 1834. The commitment to Bible translation extended even to languages that most people in the West had never heard of. For example, Robert Moffatt (1795–1883) dedicated more than forty years of his life (1826–1870) to the people of Kuruman (modern-day Botswana), including translating the entire Bible into Sechuana between 1840 and 1857. These are but a few examples of what collectively amounted to a dramatic rise in the availability of vernacular Bible translations. During the Great Century alone, more than four hundred new language groups received either the

New Testament or the entire Bible in their language. This commitment to Bible translation continues to the present day. Currently, the New Testament or the entire Bible is available in more than fifteen hundred languages! An additional nearly one thousand languages have at least one book of the Bible in their language.

The legacy of Bible translation cannot be heralded as the triumph of any one person or denomination. Instead, the Reformation brought about a theological correction that, as it turned out, unleashed one of the great periods in the history of the church. The Protestant commitment to Bible translation led to hundreds of new translations, which provided the basis for indigenous expressions of Christianity all over the world.

CHAPTER 10

The Legacy of Women Missionaries

The role of women in the mission of the church is one of the great chapters in the life of the church. In fact, the female missionaries transcended the church's debate about the role of women in clerical roles. Protestant women served as missionaries with the English Anglicans, the Dutch Reformed, the Swiss Pietists, the Norwegian Lutherans, and the American Baptists, to name a few. All of these groups have very different views about clerical authority and the role of women, as well as a variety of attitudes about marriage and social and cultural practices that impact women's role on the mission field. Nevertheless, if we focus on the role of Protestant women in missions over the entire period from 1792 to 1910, there are several amazing trends that can be observed.

Mobilization and Support

As noted earlier, the birth of the Protestant missionary society created a separate structure that was distinct from the traditional, fixed power base of church governance in the nineteenth century. Leadership in the mission society was not restricted to ordained clergy. This had enormous implications for women in ministry. Even though the formal structure of the society had male leadership, women were often the lifeblood of the society in organizing meetings, recruiting missionaries, raising funds, mobilizing prayer, and, in time, teaching about missions.

Professional Employees

As the work of missions grew, there were many new kinds of professional positions that needed to be filled. For example, nurses and teachers were needed for mission hospitals and schools. In Roman Catholic missions these roles had traditionally been filled by special orders of missionary nuns. Protestant missions, beginning in 1865, began to recruit women to fill certain specialized roles. This is an important development because, for the first time, women now had official, salaried roles within the mission that were not directly related to the work of their husbands.

Pioneer Missionaries

The year 1865, right at the heart of the Great Century, is often cited as a watershed in the history of women in missions. This is the year that Hudson Taylor founded the China Inland Mission. This mission represented a dramatic shift in missionary recruitment and service, with important implications for women. As a Brethren, Taylor did not believe in ordination and, therefore, was eager to mobilize as many lay missionaries as possible. Taylor was the first Protestant leader of a mission to directly recruit women as full missionaries in their own right. Because the China Inland Mission (CIM) was a "faith mission," there were no financial support concerns that had often hindered the denominational efforts from recognizing women as full-fledged missionaries. Single women received the same training as the men. The women were not just permitted to preach; they were expected to. Drawing from working-class peoples, men and women who were prepared to live by faith and face new challenges became part of the missions ethos from the beginning. Taylor founded the CIM while on furlough in England and returned in 1865 with the first fifteen missionary recruits, seven of whom were single women.

Many of the new faith mission societies that had been inspired by Taylor's CIM also actively recruited women as full-fledged missionaries. Mission organizations such as the North Africa Mission, the Gospel Missionary Union, and the Algiers Mission Band all mobilized more women than men for cross-cultural service. In fact, Lilias Trotter, the well-known artist-missionary to the Islamic world, was the founder of the Algiers Mission Band, making her the earliest Protestant woman to found and lead a mission society.

Taylor's pioneering effort to mobilize and send out single, female missionaries was also followed by the earlier mainstream societies. For example, in 1866 the London Missionary Society authorized an auxiliary organization known as the Ladies' Board to train women candidates and to help place them in the mission field. In the same year, the Society for Propagating the Gospel (SPG) set up an auxiliary structure known as the Ladies' Association, which was also solely for the purpose of recruiting female missionaries. An advertising pamphlet used later by the SPG to recruit women gave several reasons why women were needed on the mission field. The pamphlet, quite naturally, pointed out the need for professional qualifications, especially in medicine, nursing, and teaching. However, in an early foreshadowing of what is today called "friendship evangelism," the SPG also stressed the relational skills of women. The pamphlet stated that in the work of evangelism, women were needed to form friendships with educated women in China, Japan, and India. The relational skills of women were essential for the success of the mission. These auxiliary societies were soon followed up by mission societies solely dedicated to mobilizing women. By the end of the nineteenth century, there were more than forty women's mission societies in the United States alone, and by 1910, the end of the Great Century, the number of women outnumbered the men in Protestant missions.

Few women embodied the new possibilities for the single, female pioneer missionary as did Charlotte "Lottie" Moon (1840–1912), sometimes called the "patron saint" of Baptist missions. Lottie and her sister were teachers in a school for girls in Cartersville, Georgia. When the door opened for single women to become missionaries, Lottie applied, was accepted, and arrived in China in 1873 as a Southern Baptist missionary. After twelve years in China serving in fairly traditional roles, Lottie decided to move from Tengzhou to the interior city of Pingtu more than a hundred miles away and start her own work. This was the first time that a single female had ever started a new mission work in China. Moon eventually saw hundreds of Chinese come to the Lord, and her ministry led to the establishment of more than thirty new Chinese churches. Over the next twenty years, thousands of new believers were baptized, making Pingtu one of the greatest evangelistic centers in all of China for the Southern Baptists. Moon worked tirelessly, spending several months each year doing evangelism in villages and the rest of her time training new missionaries and writing influential articles and opinion pieces published in Southern Baptist mission magazines back in the United States. She encouraged Southern Baptist women to organize mission societies to fund and recruit more missionaries. In 1887, Moon wrote to the *Foreign Mission Journal* and proposed that the Sunday before Christmas be set aside for a special offering for missions. This annual offering, today known as the Lottie Moon Christmas

Offering, remains the largest single annual offering for missions in history, with the annual amount today exceeding $20 million.

Lottie gave her life for the sake of the gospel. At the end of her life, it was discovered that she had been giving her food rations to Chinese Christians who were suffering during a famine sweeping across China at that time. Doctors discovered that her sacrifice had led to extreme malnourishment, and she was placed on board a ship to return home so she could receive medical care. However, she died on Christmas Eve in 1912, while still aboard the ship. The first Christmas offering enabled three new missionaries to come to China. Today, her life story, along with the Christmas offering, have helped to inspire, recruit, and support thousands of new missionaries. Furthermore, men and women alike continue to be inspired by her dedication and sacrifice. Although Lottie Moon was only four feet, three inches tall, she has cast a long and influential shadow on the entire modern missionary movement.

As a father of a single, female missionary who serves in Tanzania, I am perhaps more aware than others of how Lottie Moon's story is just one of countless women who continue to shape and to serve the missionary movement of the church even today.

CHAPTER 11

Indigenous Ingenuity: Church Planting in the Great Century

One of the mistakes that is often made about the spread of the gospel around the world is the idea that the job is to just evangelize people and create avenues for them to respond to the gospel. This is why we see so many massive rallies and public events around the world where people are asked to come forward or raise their hands. This is, of course, wonderful. However, what happens the day after the rally?

The real strategic work is the planting of churches and the incorporation of new believers into churches.

No two people have helped the church to think more about this problem than the two towering missionary statesmen of the nineteenth century, Rufus Anderson (1796–1880) and Henry Venn (1796–1873). Anderson and Venn affirmed the need for people without Christ to hear the gospel and the importance of individual conversion. However, they also wisely understood that, in the long run, conversions will not last, nor will the missions movement succeed unless there is an emphasis on church planting. Venn and Anderson wrote extensively and were particularly critical of only transferring Western denominations around the world.

Venn and Anderson were also leaders in asking other important questions: What role should missionaries have in leading a new church? When is the best time for the missionaries to turn things over to the new believers? These are very important and difficult questions. These two leaders developed what would eventually become the most famous three measurements for knowing when a church was ready to stand on its own. The three measures were: self-governing, self-supporting, and self-propagating. Venn and Anderson were both convinced that reliance on foreign missionaries and foreign funding hindered the long-term growth of the church. Therefore, they were committed to training and ordaining indigenous pastors who would be supported by the new Christians. As early as 1841, Anderson made the case (which has been repeated often in our time) that the cost of supporting twenty-five missionary families from America was the same amount needed to educate a thousand natives and support two hundred as pastors.

The growing commitment to plant churches on the mission field (not just evangelize) led, over time, to a stunning variety of churches being planted on the mission field. Some of the new churches were intentionally planted as "daughter" churches, which remained financially and administratively dependent on the "mother" church in the West. Other new churches were organized into some kind of new national association with varying levels of dependence and association with the sending body. Still other new Christian movements organized themselves into indigenous churches that were organizationally autonomous from the church of the missionary. An analysis of the details of the explosive number of church plants during the nineteenth century would be impossible. However, to capture a small sense of the sheer scale of the new church planting, two former colleagues of mine have documented 1,488 separate denominations or church movements that emerged between 1792 and 1910. This represents hundreds of thousands of new Christians throughout every inhabited continent.

An examination of where Christians were located in 1792 and in 1910 is very revealing. While the dramatic growth of Christianity in the Majority World takes place in the twentieth century, it is the nineteenth century that planted the seeds for that growth. In 1792, 98 percent of all Protestant Christians lived in the Western world. By the end of the nineteenth century, small, but vibrant groups of Christians were found in many countries all around the world. For example, the 176,000 Christians in Nigeria in 1900 or the 92,000 Christians in Tanzania may seem tiny by today's standards of Christianity in Africa. Today, Nigeria has more than 64 million Christians and Tanzania has 20 million. But the point is that the church was planted, and planted widely. Of course, Christianity did not always grow and prosper in the wake of the missionary labors of the Great Century. Morocco, for example, had more than 30,000 Christians at the end of the nineteenth century, but since that time, the number of Christians in Morocco continues to decline as a percentage of overall population.[1]

Nevertheless, looking back on the whole sweep of the Great Century, one must recognize that it represented a remarkable advance of church planting around the world. Never before in history had so many new expressions of the church emerged in so many places. Today there are more than forty thousand separate church movements in the world!

CHAPTER 12

Global Collaboration: The Birth of World Christianity

The fifth and final theme that helps to capture something of the vibrancy in the nineteenth century is the first World Missionary Conference, which was held in Edinburgh, Scotland, on June 14–23, 1910.

The climate that led to the Edinburgh conference in 1910 can, perhaps, best be summed up by the publication of John Mott's *The Evangelization of the World in This Generation*.

John Mott (1865–1955) was a great mission mobilizer, having founded and chaired the Student Volunteer Movement from 1888 to 1920, as well as serving as the traveling secretary of the YMCA (1888–1915). Thousands of students came through these movements and joined the ranks of the mission societies to serve cross-culturally. Over the course of his work, Mott traveled nearly two million miles, gaining a great deal of firsthand knowledge about the work of missions around the world. Mott became convinced that with better coordination and strategic thinking, the entire world could be evangelized in one generation. This led to the publication of Mott's book in 1900, which sparked a wave of optimism about fulfilling the Great Commission in that generation. The book also highlighted the need for greater cooperation among the many mission agencies and more strategic thinking about the entire missionary enterprise. The conference in Edinburgh was designed to organize the final push for world evangelization. John R. Mott was named the chair of the event.

From the perspective of the twenty-first century, it would be easy to dismiss the conference as overly audacious in thinking they could plan for and organize the evangelization of the entire world. However, from the perspective of the early twentieth century, it was meticulously planned to be the most globally representative event in history. Rather than inviting delegates from churches, with their potential endless theological debates and ecclesiastical divisions, the invitations went out to every known mission society that was working with non-Christian peoples. The societies were invited to send delegates based on a strict proportionality to the size and scope of the work of the missions organization. Thus, although the ethnic origin of most of the delegates was of European descent, they came, quite literally, from all over the world, bringing extensive, firsthand experience of the mission field.

The conference was organized thematically, with each day of the conference centered on one of the following themes:

1. Carrying the Gospel to All the Non-Christian World
2. The Church in the Mission Field
3. Education in Relation to the Christianization of National Life
4. Missionary Message in Relation to the Non-Christian World
5. The Preparation of Missionaries
6. The Home Base of Missions
7. Missions and Governments
8. Cooperation and the Promotion of Unity[1]

These eight themes shed light on what were considered the most important issues and concerns of the day. Themes one, four, and six highlight how dramatically the world has changed in the last century. In 1910 it seemed entirely plausible to divide the world into the "Christian" and "non-Christian" spheres, with the West representing the "Christian" world, and the Majority World the "non-Christian" world. In 1910, the "home base" of missions was, undoubtedly, the Western world. Today, such assumptions are no longer tenable. Theme two ("The Church in the Mission Field") reflects the hunger for accurate information about the state of the church in the Majority World. Themes three and five reveal the long-term value of education in Protestant missions. Themes four and seven highlight the importance of understanding the challenges and issues raised by followers of Hinduism, Buddhism, and Islam, as well as the political contexts into which religion is embedded and that dramatically influence the missionary encounter. The last theme highlights the need for cooperation and collaboration as we collectively understand our shared roles in participating in God's mission.

In conclusion, from the perspective of 2016, looking back on the legacy of the 1910 World Missionary Conference in Edinburgh, there are several key features that capture the legacy of the conference. *First, Edinburgh 1910 initiated an entirely new structure and constituency for reflecting on Christianity in the world.* By focusing on delegates from the mission societies rather than the churches themselves, they were able to bring together people who were personally engaged in missionary work and who understood the challenges that faced the church at that time. By making it a "working" conference, rather than a motivational or inspirational event, the delegates were required to read and prepare a considerable amount of material before arriving at the conference. Therefore, those who came were prepared for a serious engagement of important issues.

Second, Edinburgh 1910 marked the real birth of mission studies as a serious thing the church gives thought to. Today, for example, we have very detailed books, such as the *Atlas of Global Christianity*, or the *World Christian Encyclopedia*, which gives very detailed information about the world and where Christians are located, and so forth.

Finally, over the course of the ten-day conference, there was a growing realization and recognition that Christianity was a truly worldwide movement. Never again could the Western church think honestly about the Christian movement in isolation from vibrant currents of indigenous Christianity around the world. Edinburgh 1910 was truly a turning point in the history of world Christianity. It is one of the great ironies of history that at a conference held in the heart of old Europe, the church, for the first time, captured a glimpse of a world-wide church.

As problems in the Western church seem to mount, it is encouraging to remember that we are part of a worldwide fellowship of Christians from around the world! It is not unusual for delegates from the countries of Africa to lovingly remind Western pastors of the gospel and the heritage we commonly share. This is one of the great strengths of being a part of a global movement.

Act Three

The Flowering of World Christianity, 1910–Present

Introduction

Most of us have become accustomed to seeing a wide range of new translations and specialty Bibles now widely available. The King James "Authorized Version," once the only Bible available for the English speaker, has been eclipsed by dozens of new translations, paraphrases, study Bibles, and special focus Bibles. In addition to translations such as the RSV, NASB, NIV, and NEB, we can now read translations and paraphrased Bibles especially for children, for youth, and so forth. So, perhaps it is not too much to ask you to imagine another remarkable and unusual kind of Bible. Rather than a Bible that is in only one language, imagine a Bible that has the amazing ability to reflect the languages that Christians around the world speak, in the actual proportion to how they are globally represented.

If this Bible had been held by a Christian in 1910 who was attending the World Missionary Conference in Edinburgh, the majority of the Bible would be in English and a few other western European languages. However, if that same Bible were to be opened one century later, in 2010, it would be a vastly different Bible. You would read this imaginary Bible in Spanish from Genesis 1 all the way through the third chapter of Joshua, since Spanish now represents the most spoken language of world Christianity. The Bible would then become English and continue in English from Joshua 4 all the way to 1 Kings 6. Then, quite surprisingly, the Bible would become Chinese from 1 Kings 6 through 2 Chronicles 14. The language changes would start to appear more regularly, including major sections of the New Testament in Korean,

Hindi, and Swahili. By the time you reached Revelation, the Bible would start to change languages almost every verse, and then by every word, until all of the 2,251 languages spoken by Christians around the world would find their place in this imaginary Bible. I don't know how useful this Bible would be, but it would dramatically illustrate the central theme of this third act of our play, namely, the full emergence of the diversity of vibrant Christianity in so many different parts of the world. The global expansion of the church of Jesus Christ is widely regarded as the single most important development in the history of the church of the twentieth century.

The purpose of act 3 is to cast a historical light on the emergence and flowering of Christianity as a world movement. As noted in act 1 (missions before 1792) and act 2 (1792–1910), a full survey of the period from 1910 to the present is not possible without reducing the period to an almost mindless barrage of statistics and data. Therefore, to capture something of the grandeur and spirit of twentieth-century missions, we will focus on another seven pictures around which I will share seven brief stories or vignettes of world Christianity. These representative stories are taken from Africa, Latin America, the Middle East, three parts of Asia, and Europe. The following stories will be examined:

1. the growth of Pentecostalism in Latin America;

2. the African indigenous churches in Sub-Saharan Africa;

3. Muslims who are following Christ in the mosque;

4. South Indian missionaries to Hindus in North India;

5. non-registered "house church" movements in China;

6. the Korean missionary movement; and

7. vibrant European churches emerging out of post-Christian Europe.

Each story should be seen as illustrative of the much larger story of global Christianity.

CHAPTER 13

Pentecostalism in Latin America

Although Pentecostalism is a global phenomenon with adherents in nearly every country in the world, our first story of global Christianity focuses on Latin American Pentecostalism as representative of a larger global phenomenon in world Christianity. Traditionally, when we think of the church, we think of it in terms of three big blocks: Roman Catholic, Protestant, and Eastern Orthodox. Today, there are thousands of new Christian movements that are both independent and Pentecostal that cannot be traced back to the sixteenth-century Reformation. In fact, this is by far the fastest-growing segment of Christianity around the world.

How big is it? Well, today there are more than a half a billion adherents; it is second only to Roman Catholicism as the largest single block of Christian identity. Roman Catholic missionaries began to arrive in Latin America in the late fifteenth century after the Padroado. Over the next few centuries Latin America became one of the most thoroughly Roman Catholic regions in the world. Protestant missionaries did not arrive until the late nineteenth century, and Pentecostalism did not come to Latin America until the early decades of the twentieth century. Yet, after only seventy-five years in Central and South America, Pentecostals make up three-quarters of all Latin American Protestants. This is important to recognize because the vast majority of what is called "Protestant" or "independent" or "indigenous" growth in Latin America is made up of Pentecostals. As early as 1962, *Time* magazine declared Pentecostalism to be the fastest-growing church in the

Western Hemisphere. The growth rate is now three times faster than population growth.

It is not uncommon to hear the criticism that Pentecostalism is "a mile wide and an inch deep." While this is an important concern, we cannot ignore the vibrant life of this new branch of Christianity in Latin America that is almost without parallel and exceeds the growth rate of Protestantism in central Europe during the time of the Reformation. This transformation deserves our attention.

It has taken a long time for North American historians and theologians to take seriously either the global Pentecostal movement or any critique it might offer to our own theology. As late as 1968, William McLoughlin contributed a chapter to *Religion in America* entitled "Is There a Third Force in Christendom?" where he dismissed the Pentecostal movement as a passing "effluvia." He predicted that "the pietistic upthrust by fringe-sect dissenters and come-outers does not in itself constitute the creation of a significant new religious movement in Christendom." He went on to say that

Pentecostalism does "not constitute a dynamic new force capable of replacing or seriously threatening the old order."[1] What McLoughlin failed to realize is that the very thing he predicted would not happen had, in fact, *already happened*! By 1968 the global shift, while yet unrecognized, had already occurred and the old structures of Christianity were passing away. The shift happened swiftly and dramatically because at the same time that Pentecostals around the world were in the process of rediscovering the vibrancy of historic Christian faith, the mainline churches were largely abandoning it, losing members by the millions and thereby accelerating their move to the sidelines of American religious life.

This snapshot is a picture of an array of vibrant new movements in Latin America that broadly fall under the category of "Pentecostal." Pentecostals believe that the Holy Spirit exhibits the same signs and wonders He did in the first century. They believe in divine healing. Some may believe in prophecies or words of knowledge whereby the Holy Spirit directs the church today. A worship service may be very exuberant, with people lifting their hands or shouting praises to God during the worship. Many who may be reading this little book will look at this picture of these new movements and ask, "What does this mean for us?" If you belong to a mainline church, such as a Presbyterian or a United Methodist or an Episcopal church, it is very difficult to imagine a day when these churches no longer constitute the major blocks of Christianity in the United States. However, many of the same forces of new church planting are taking place in the United States. Indeed, all of the traditional mainline churches are in significant decline and are being replaced by newer movements that have a very different history and orientation. In short, the face of Christianity is changing both here and around the world.

I believe that if the mainline churches are to be renewed, they will need to listen carefully to these new movements, which hold to a high view of Scripture, believe passionately in evangelism, and have a deep commitment to the centrality of Jesus Christ and the power of the Holy Spirit.

CHAPTER 14

The African Indigenous Churches in Sub-Saharan Africa

Our second picture is of a group of African Christians worshipping God. The last half of the twentieth century and the early decades of the twenty-first century have turned out to be the genesis of a new Christian awakening in Africa. For example, in the last three decades of the twentieth century, the overall percentage of African Christians rose from around 25 percent of the population to about 46 percent, which amounts to

8.4 million new Christians every year.[1] If you are having a hard time getting your head around that number, just think 23,000 new Christians per day, every day, for decades!

Much of this Christian awakening in Africa remains securely within the Roman Catholic, Anglican, and Protestant churches, which remained after the end of colonization. For example, as recently as 1955 the Roman Catholic Church cited only 16 million members on the entire African continent, compared with more than 150 million Roman Catholics in Africa today. It is estimated that by 2025 this number will blossom to around 230 million.[2] Similar growth has been cited among Anglicans in Africa. For example, the number of Anglicans in Nigeria alone is now approaching the number of Anglicans in England, the traditional heartland of Anglicanism. The shifting center of gravity within Anglicanism has important implications for the future of the worldwide Anglican community, and has been regularly cited, for example, in the recent struggles within the Episcopalian Church in the United States, where churches

opposed to departures from historic orthodoxy have sepa-
rated from their Episcopalian bishop and submitted to the
authority of an African bishop.

Methodism has also grown substantially in Africa. For
example, between 1970 and 2005 the Methodists in Nigeria
grew from 80,000 to more than 2 million. As a point of
comparison, it should be noted that during that same time
period, the Methodists in the United Kingdom lost more
than half of their entire membership (2 million to 996,000)
and the United Methodist Church in the United States lost
7 million members, dropping from 14 million down to 8
million members.[3] There is no doubt that many of the most
controversial votes, which would have further eroded the
United Methodist commitment to historic faith, were turned
back because of the growing influence of African Methodists.

In addition to the African renewal of the older Christian
movements, there has also been a dramatic growth in
independent or indigenous churches. These new church
movements are sometimes known collectively as the AIC,

which is an acronym for African Independent Churches or, alternatively, African Indigenous Churches. There is no single movement known as AIC. Rather, this is a broad term representing more than sixty million churches that belong to more than ten thousand distinct African denominations or smaller movements. These are churches founded by Africans and are for Africans.

Causes in the Emergence of the AIC

There are three main reasons why AIC churches have emerged, although not all three of these apply equally to all AIC. *First, the rise of nationalism in the post-colonial period stimulated the need for churches established or led by Africans.* Some of the AIC are highly structured and hierarchal movements, whereas others are more informal and lay oriented. Nevertheless, all of the AIC emphasize the importance of African leadership within their respective movements. *Second, AIC churches seek to reflect African cultural forms and pride in their African identity and heritage.* In some cases earnest attempts were made to accommodate traditional African practices and customs. In other cases, as we observed in Gregory the Great's advice to Augustine, alternative Christian practices were set in place to help separate Africans from what are regarded as unbiblical customs and practices. In both cases, these churches demonstrate their awareness of the indigenous context. *Finally, the AIC generally emphasizes doctrinal themes or practices that were felt to be neglected or in error in the various expressions of Christianity that had been imported into Africa from the West.* These themes often include a greater emphasis on personal holiness and/or the role of the Holy Spirit in the Christian life. Many churches within the AIC point out that the Western missionaries did not take the spirit world or demons seriously enough. They often pointed out how the ministry of Jesus was characterized by supernatural healing and demonic deliverance, whereas the missionaries largely interpreted disease in a scientific and rationalistic way, and relied more on hospitals than on prayer. Others feel that greater doctrinal clarity was needed on a wide range of other issues as well, including marriage and gender issues, the Christian response to poverty, and the environment.

Even this brief survey should make it clear that the sheer size and diversity of African Christianity makes it impossible to generalize about the theology and practice of Christianity in Africa. Many of these churches reflect biblical orthodoxy, are Christocentric, and have a high regard for the Scriptures. In reflecting on these movements, it is important to remember that sometimes what are cited as heretical practices by Western writers are either neutral cultural expressions of Christianity or are the restoration of certain features of biblical Christianity that have been neglected by some Western expressions of Christianity. There are, of course, plenty of examples of quasi-orthodox and heretical beliefs, practices, or tendencies that have been incorporated into various expressions of African Christianity. However, we can no longer afford to ignore the voices and experiences of African Christians, since Africa will soon become the most Christian continent on earth.

CHAPTER 15

Muslims Who Are Following Christ

Our next photograph is of a group of former Muslims who are following Jesus Christ as Savior and Lord. When reflecting on the emergence of global Christianity, there is a natural tendency to focus exclusively on the large mega-movements comprising millions of new followers of Christ. However, it is important to remember that all of these large movements started as small, marginalized events that, at the time, were not appreciated or recognized for their significance. In chapter 13, for example, we surveyed the dramatic development of global Pentecostalism, which, along with charismatic movements, now comprises 600 million people worldwide. However, at the 1910 World Missionary Conference (which we explored in chapter 12) in Edinburgh, it received virtually no attention at all, even though dramatic movements of the Holy Spirit had already taken place in Wales (1904–1905), on Azusa Street in the United States (1906–1909), in India (1906), in Korea (1907), in China (1908), and in Africa (Ivory Coast, Ghana, and Nigeria, 1908–1914).

Thus, it important to be attentive to movements that may be quite small numerically, but remain important, strategic breakthroughs and could, in time, become major developments in the world Christian movement. For this reason the focus of the third story of global Christianity will be a small, but important Christian movement that is quietly occurring in the Islamic world.

The Islamic world has long been considered one of the most challenging places for Christian witness. This is partly because of distorted understandings of Christians and the Christian gospel throughout the Islamic world. For example, one missionary tells the story of a Kuwaiti Muslim who was asked what he knew about Christians and Christianity. He replied that a Christian is someone who promotes immorality, pornography, and sexually oriented television programs like *Sex in the City*, *Desperate Housewives*, and so on. This may shock us, but Muslims assume that the religion and the state are united. Therefore, anything that is in Western culture is assumed to be an expression of Christian ideals and faith. I have encountered this perception many times over the years as I have interacted with Muslims in India or other parts of the world.

Yet, despite these perceptions about Christianity, Muslims generally hold very positive views of Jesus Christ. You may not know this, but the Qur'an has more than forty references to Jesus Christ. For example, the Qur'an teaches that Jesus had a miraculous birth and that He was a miracle worker. It also teaches that Jesus was a prophet and He was without sin. Of course, there are many very important doctrines of the Christian faith that Muslims do not affirm (such as the eternality of Jesus Christ, His deity, His bodily resurrection, and so forth). Nevertheless, Muslims generally have a positive view of Christ, even if they do not accept the full biblical teachings about Christ.

These positive views of Christ alongside such embarrassing perceptions regarding words such as *Christian*, *church*, and *Christianity* within the Muslim community have led some Muslims to become followers of Jesus, but remain in the mosque rather than unite with any Christian church. They do this for several reasons. First, they sometimes find that Christians do not trust them because there is so much fear of persecution in the Islamic world. When someone meets a person who is from an Islamic family who claims they are now following Christ, there can be some suspicion and fear. Second, we have discovered that many Muslims who seem resistant to the gospel are actually not rejecting the gospel per se, but Westernized forms, distortions, and misunderstandings of Christianity that Muslims find repugnant. These reasons have given rise to new churches only for people with an Islamic background. Some of these churches will use Islamic terms for God (Allah), prayer (*salat*), and the Gospels (*Injil*). Likewise, these churches might embrace outward practices normally associated with Islamic faithfulness, such as avoiding pork, abstaining from alcohol, removing shoes when coming to worship, or fasting during the month of Ramadan. They might call themselves "followers of Isa" (the Islamic name for Jesus).

All of this seems quite strange to us, but God is moving in the Islamic world. Thousands of Muslims are coming to Christ, and they are starting to gather in churches, even if they have to meet in secret. It is not uncommon for Western people to worry about Islam and be fearful of Muslims because of recent acts of terrorism perpetuated in the name of Islam. However, the church has always had the same answer to fears like this: perfect love casts out all fear. There are thousands of Christians who live throughout the Islamic world who have loved many, many Muslims into the kingdom of God. We saw this in chapter 4 with the life of Raymond Lull. It is still true today. There are many ways people can throw up a defense against Christian teachings. But there has never been a defense against radical, sacrificial love. As we love people, they are drawn to Jesus Christ. This is happening in unprecedented ways around the Islamic world.

CHAPTER 16

South Indian Missionaries to North India

Our fourth picture is of a group of Indian Christians from southern India who are moving to North India to become missionaries. Does this sound odd? After all, when we think of missionaries, we often think about Westerners traveling to faraway countries to preach the gospel and plant churches. One of the most important developments in the history of modern missions has been the emergence of growing numbers of missionaries from Latin America, Africa, and Asia. This fourth picture of world Christianity focuses on Indian missionaries from South India who are crossing cultural and linguistic barriers to bring the gospel to North India.

In chapter 2 we explored the early roots of Christianity in India through the apostle Thomas who arrived in India in AD 52 and, according to tradition, started seven churches. These Christians remained small and culturally isolated in India until, as we explored, more and more Christian groups began to arrive. What I didn't tell you in chapter 2 was that almost all of these missionaries were working and living in South India. The result is that over the centuries Christianity developed a fairly strong foothold in South India, but there were far fewer Christians in North India. But in 1839 a German missionary named Herman Gundert (1814–1893) arrived in South India (the state of Kerala) and produced a well-received translation of the Bible in the local language known as Malayalam.

You will recall that in chapter 9 we explored the importance of these Bible translations. Well, this Bible translation
spawned a number of renewal movements in South India.
One of the most important occurred in 1859 and was led
by Abraham Malpān (1796–1843), known as the "Martin
Luther of the East." Malpān was deeply influenced by the
Anglican missionaries and their regard for the Bible. This
led Malpān to lead a group of reformers within the Syrian
Orthodox Church in Kerala to test all things by the Bible
and to reject any customs or ceremonies not authorized by
Scripture. Like Martin Luther of old, on the eve of a sacred
festival, Malpān seized an image of a saint used in the well-
known (and lucrative) festival and threw it into a well,
stirring up rage among the pilgrims. He then presented a
manifesto of twenty-three corrupt practices in the faith and
life of the church that he considered unbiblical. He advocated many mainstream evangelical principles, including
the authority of Scripture and justification by faith alone.
The reformers were expelled, Malpān was excommunicated,

and they eventually formed an independent church. But the movement could not be stopped. The evangelical emphasis on preaching, justification by faith, and the authority of Scripture led, over the years, to at least thirty distinct reform movements. The result was a growing burden for the lost and a desire to bring the gospel to North India, where, comparatively, there were so few Christians. These movements continue to the present day.

I would like to focus on one example of a ministry in North India I have had the privilege of observing for the last twenty years. Our focus will be on the ministry of Bharat Susamachar Samiti, founded by George Chavanikamannil in 1987. George Chavanikamannil was born in Kerala in 1948 and grew up in the Syrian Orthodox Church. While in college he was exposed to evangelical teachings and was called to be a missionary to North India. Although he immigrated to the United States to receive theological training and, eventually to work for World Vision, he never forgot his call to North India. He eventually decided to return to India and relocate to North India as a missionary. One day, he took out a calculator and, after a few calculations, determined that even if he were to preach to five thousand people every day, it would take him nearly three centuries to preach the gospel to everyone in India. He realized the importance of multiplying laborers for the harvest, based on Jesus' words in Matthew 9:37 that "the harvest is plentiful but the workers are few." Therefore, he decided to start a training school to equip hundreds of new laborers for the task. The New Theological College was officially opened in 1989 and over the last twenty years has equipped and trained hundreds of Indians, from both North and South, to plant churches in North India. A sister organization, known as Christian Evangelistic Assemblies (CEA), was also founded to help coordinate and support graduates who focused on church planting. In less than two decades, graduates working through the CEA have planted more than five hundred churches in North India, mostly among Hindu-background believers. The central training center in Dehradun, Uttarakhand, in North India is supported by ten regional training centers strategically located across North India for the purposes of discipleship, ongoing training, and supervision. The church-planting ministry has also invested considerable resources into practical development in India, including schools, orphanages, literacy centers, job training, and a wide range of other ministries. This ministry, along with dozens of other, similar ministries founded by South Indians, is collectively having a dramatic impact on the growth of Christianity in what is known as the "Hindi belt," long considered one of the most challenging mission fields in the world.

CHAPTER 17

The Non-Registered House Church Movement in China

October 1, 1949, marks the victory of the Communists in China under the leadership of Mao Zedong and the emergence of the People's Republic of China. In the first year of the Communist rule, thousands of foreign missionaries were forced out of China. It is estimated that in 1949 there were approximately four million Christians in the entirety of China. The new Communist leadership declared their unequivocal opposition to all theistic religions, insisting instead on the worship of the state, especially the personality cult of Mao Zedong, known simply as Chairman Mao.

In 1951 the Communist Party set up the Religious Affairs Bureau to oversee and supervise what it anticipated to be the final death throes of theistic religion in China. When the rapid demise of religion did not occur, the Chinese government opted for a policy of draconian control. The Protestant churches were controlled through an official government body eventually known as the Three Self Patriotic Movement (TSPM). The TSPM closed the majority of churches and forced all pastors in China to acknowledge that Christianity in China had largely been used as a force for imperialism and Western aggression against China. The TSPM claimed that the legacy of Protestant missions in China was of a church divided hopelessly into a multitude of denominations. The TSPM ostensibly sought to unite the church under a single "patriotic" banner. Any pastor who refused to sign a statement of patriotic loyalty to China, which included a denunciation of any Christian expressions other than those registered by the TSPM and controlled by the Religious Affairs Bureau, would result in imprisonment, beating, and public shaming.

During the Cultural Revolution (1966–1976), Chairman Mao stepped up the official hostility toward Christianity by promoting the destruction of church buildings, the confiscation of church property, and the disenfranchisement of all public expressions of faith. The arrogant assumption of Communist leaders who maintained that Christianity would perish in China was reflected in the headline of the *South China Morning Post* in August 1966, which proudly declared, "Christianity in Shangai Comes to an End." As it turned out, this was hardly the case.

Throughout these early decades of Communist rule in China, God raised up a number of prominent Chinese dissidents, such as Wang Mingdao (1900–1991), Allen Yuan (1914–2005), and Moses Xie (b. 1918), who remained faithful to the gospel and steadfastly refused to register with the TSPM. Each of these men spent at least two decades in prison and were repeatedly intimidated, beaten, and interrogated by Chinese authorities because of their faith in Jesus Christ. Other famous dissidents who spent decades in prison were Watchman Nee (1903–1972) and Samuel Lamb (b. 1925). These leaders also opposed the politicization of the church and wrote many Christian books, pamphlets, and hymns that helped to foster and nurture networks of non-registered house churches completely independent of the state-controlled church.

The amazing truth is that despite all of this aggression against the church, there continues to be a steady, and even dramatic, growth in the non-registered "house church" movement in China. That is the picture I want to show you—a picture of a Chinese house church. Ironically, the government's forced separation of the Chinese church from outside associations actually helped to further stimulate indigenous Christianity, which was not associated with or dependent on foreign funds, personnel, or initiatives. The result was an explosion of the independent, non-registered churches in China, which appears to be impacting almost every segment of Chinese society. While estimates vary, there are probably more than ninety million Christians in China today, making it one of the fastest-growing churches in the world. It is from these new Chinese Christians, mostly found in non-registered churches, that a remarkable missionary thrust is emerging. We now predict that by the year 2025, China will be sending out more foreign missionaries to other countries than any other nation. These missionaries will not be formally trained and sent missionaries in the way we often think about the missionary force. Rather, it will be the quiet scattering of thousands and thousands of believers across central Asia and around the world bearing witness to Jesus Christ.

Truly, the dramatic growth of the church in China and the growing collective force of these new missionaries will likely be the most important story of the twenty-first-century church. It should also encourage those of us who are often deeply worried about Christian persecution and the future of the church. The lesson of history is that the more the church suffers, the stronger it becomes. Truly, the light of the gospel cannot be put out!

CHAPTER 18

The Korean Missionary Movement

Despite the relatively late origin of Christianity in Korea, as explored in chapter 7, Korean Christianity has experienced remarkable growth. In fact, South Korea is widely regarded as the home of the modern church growth movement, which is exemplified by the remarkable story of the Yoido Full Gospel church founded by Dr. David Cho. Begun in 1958 with only five people in a small living room, the church now claims more than 700,000 members, making it easily the largest church in the world. Today, there are more than 15 million Christians in South Korea alone, belonging to around 47,000 churches, making it one of the most important centers of Asian Christianity. The focus of this picture is on the modern Korean missionary movement, which has distinguished itself as one of the fastest-growing national missionary movements in the world.

The Korea Research Institute for Missions (KRIM) has conducted regular studies of the Korean missionary movement. In 1979 they reported 93 Koreans who were involved in overseas missions. This number has steadily climbed, with 1,178 serving in 1989, and 8,103 in 2000. By 2006, there were 14,905 Korean missionaries serving with 174 different mission agencies, representing a 106-fold increase in only twenty-seven years. Korean missionaries are now found in 168 different countries, but are mostly found in Asia (47 percent), especially China, Philippines, and Japan, with fewer than 6 percent serving in Latin America and fewer than 8 percent in Africa. Currently, about one thousand new missionaries are being sent out by South Korea each year, making it one of the most important new mission-sending countries in the world.[1]

Having observed the Korean missionary movement for a number of years, I have been struck by the energy and determination of the movement. One of the privileges that has come in my serving as president of Asbury Theological Seminary has been getting to know Bishop Sundo Kim, who serves on our board of trustees. Bishop Kim is the pastor of the largest Methodist church in the world. Having spent time in Korea with him, I am amazed at the depth of their faith, the fervency of their praying, and the zeal with which they take up gospel work. Even though Bishop Kim is in his eighties, he is still making plans to plant two more churches and has recently opened a ten-story social service center to meet the needs of hurting people in Korea. Whenever I spend time with Korean Christians, I always go away inspired to pray more, believe God more, and to never even think about retiring! It is truly a wonderful experience to spend time with a group of people who, in every way, help you to become a better Christian.

Looking at the movement as a whole, it is possible to make the case that Korea is the greatest missionary nation of our time. On every continent we now find Korean missionaries preaching the gospel, planting new churches, and serving the poor. In the coming years we can expect hundreds more, from Tashkent to Timbuktu, bearing witness to Jesus Christ. Indeed, the story of twenty-first-century missions can no longer be told without taking into consideration the increasingly global witness of Korean Christians.

These last two chapters are important because they help us to see that the worldwide mission of the church is not an enterprise only being carried by a few dedicated Western missionaries. It is a global enterprise. We have an important part to play, as do all nations on the earth.

CHAPTER 19

Post-Christendom European Christianity

Our final picture brings us full circle back to Europe. We often hear bad news about the church in Europe. But whenever I hear such reports, I am reminded of a comment made by Philip Jenkins: "Christianity is never as weak as it appears, nor as strong as it appears."[1] This adage is certainly true of European Christianity. One might be tempted to think that with the rise of the Majority World church and the collapse of old Christendom and the emergence of a post-Christian climate in Europe, the two words *Christianity* and *Europe* might begin to sound like an odd oxymoron.

However, there are two pictures in Europe that must be understood to complete these seven final pictures of twenty-first-century world Christianity. The first is the rise of vibrant immigrant churches in Europe that are transforming the face of Christianity within Europe and giving rise to a post-Western Christianity right in the heart of Europe. The second picture is that of ministers and priests in the older churches who are remaining faithful in the midst of the transition from Christendom to post-Christendom.

The Rise of Immigrant Churches in Western Europe

One of the most important differences between the missionaries coming from North America and those which are sent from Africa, Asia, and Latin America is how determined these new missionaries are to reach Europe for Jesus Christ. The majority of North American mission agencies are focused on the traditionally unreached people groups of the world.

In contrast, missionaries from Africa and Asia have demonstrated a sustained interest in planting churches in North America and Europe.

We do not normally think about the heartlands of old Christendom as a place for new church plants. In fact, if one drives through any major city in western Europe, it is not difficult to find large church buildings that have been closed because of dwindling, elderly congregations who are no longer able to sustain the enormous cost of keeping up such large facilities. In Denmark, for example, even though 83 percent of the population is nominally affiliated with the Lutheran state church, only 1 to 2 percent attend with any regularity.[2] The Church of Scotland, which is the official state church in Scotland, now has fewer than 500,000 members in the entire country.[3] In 2005, George Carey, the former archbishop of Canterbury, gave an address entitled "A Faith for a Confused and Challenging Time," in which he said that if the Church of England were a human being, "the last rites would be administered at any moment."[4] These statements and statistics are now commonplace. However, if you live in Europe, perhaps the most obvious sign of these troubles is seeing how so many of these churches have been transformed into housing flats, theaters, public halls, and businesses. For example, just below the historic castle in Edinburgh, at the top of the Royal Mile, is the site of the former Church of Scotland Assembly Hall and the former home of the Highland Church of Scotland. Its spire towers over Edinburgh and is the highest point in the city. Today, however, the church is closed and it is now the center for the annual Edinburgh cultural festival. Hundreds of examples like this could be cited all across the United Kingdom and throughout Western Europe.

It comes as a surprise, therefore, to realize that in the midst of the dramatic decline of the old state churches, there is a remarkable growth in the immigrant churches that often occurs under the radar of all of these dismal statistics. It is now estimated that there are approximately fifteen hundred missionaries from fifty nations working in the United Kingdom alone. The amazing stories of these "new" missionaries make for fascinating reading. We often think of missionary biographies that focus on Western missionaries in remote, tribal areas. The story of Marilyn Laszlo in the jungles of Papua, New Guinea, or Amy Carmichael rescuing orphan girls from a life of temple prostitution in India all fall within the comfortable parameters of what we have heretofore known as the classic missionary biography. It is more difficult to envision new, twenty-first-century missionary biographies of, for example, African missionaries planting churches in the urban West. Yet, the story of African, Brazilian, and Korean missionaries coming to Europe is the new, unfolding missionary story.

The African churches represent the largest and most visible segment of the "new Christians" of Europe. However, similar stories on a smaller scale can be found among the growing Indian, Chinese, Brazilian, Filipino, and Korean churches in Europe, to name a few. These new churches represent the new face of European Christianity. No longer can glib statements be made about the decline of Christianity in Europe without clarifying that we are referring to what is sometimes called the "old-stock white" peoples of Europe, not the growing immigrant populations, which are not part of this decline, but are increasingly building vibrant new churches right in the heart of old Christendom.

Keeping the Faith in Europe

To characterize Europe as teeming with vibrant immigrant churches growing alongside the dying historic churches would be a gross exaggeration for two reasons. *First, there are signs that the second- and third-generation members of the immigrant churches are beginning to move into the religious mainstream.* In 2005 John Sentamu, a Ugandan, was installed as the archbishop of York, widely regarded as the second most important Anglican bishopric behind only the archbishop of Canterbury. In his installation address he declared that the time had come for the church to "learn the faith afresh from the Christians of Africa and Asia."[5] In Kiev the Nigerian pastor Sunday Adelja pastors a Pentecostal congregation of thirty thousand members who are overwhelmingly white.

Second, it is important to look beyond statistics (either of growth or decline) in an assessment of the health of the church. I had the privilege of living in Europe from 1995 to 1998 and again for six months in 2008. Over the years we lived in Scotland, we moved several times, and always sought to attend a church within walking distance of our home. I had the honor of sitting under the ministries of a number of faithful pastors, such as Kevin Scott in Edinburgh, Peter Gardner in Pathhead, Mark Nicholas in Gorebridge, and Kenneth Baird in North Leith. None of these men pastor large churches, and all are serving denominations (Church of Scotland and the Scottish Episcopal Church) that are, statistically speaking, in serious decline. Yet, each of these men is faithfully preaching the gospel each week. They are quietly conducting Alpha courses, holding Bible studies, and sharing the gospel in their respective parishes. Certainly one of the most enduring lessons of the crucifixion of Christ is that God often does His most profound work under the cloak of failure.

Furthermore, all of the statistics about the decline of the *state* churches in Europe often fail to point out the rise of the independent churches in Europe, many with vibrant and growing ministries. There are Baptist, Pentecostal, and interdenominational churches all across Europe, many with growing and thriving congregations, drawing from both traditional and immigrant communities. In Edinburgh, for example, some of the largest congregations in the city would include the nondenominational Carrubbers Christian Centre, originally a D. L. Moody mission dating back to 1858, and Charlotte Chapel, an independent Baptist church located in the heart of the city.

These churches should be a great encouragement to those of us in the United States who look around with concern about the church. These European Christians are demonstrating how to be faithful to Jesus Christ in the midst of a cultural exile where the church is often regarded as an outdated icon of the past. They are learning to be missionaries in the midst of the crumbling ruins of Christendom and the emerging mission field of Europe. They have the prophetic vision to see the shallowness of Europe's great experiment with secularism and take the long view that because the gospel always retains its power, in time it will raise up better hearers.

Conclusion

This little book has carried us through two thousand years of Christian history. These snapshots have hopefully offered a few important glimpses into the unfolding work of God throughout time. Many of the most important stories will not be fully known until the full revelation of the new creation. Until then, we "see only a reflection" (1 Cor. 13:12). However, the few glimpses that we are able to discern are revealing that the global church of Jesus Christ is increasingly beginning to reflect that great eschatological vision of the apostle John where he sees men and women from every nation, tribe, people, and language worshipping the Lamb, our Lord Jesus Christ.

Notes

Chapter 3: The Tale of Two Monks

1. Norman E. Thomas, ed., *Classic Texts in Mission and World Christianity* (Maryknoll, NY: Orbis Books, 2003), 22.
2. Ibid., 11—12. For the complete text of the Xi'an Stele with a full analysis, see Jean-Pierre Charbonnier, *Christians in China* (San Francisco: Ignatius Press, 2007), 21–38.

Chapter 4: Raymond Lull and the Challenge of Islam

1. Augustus Neander, *General History of the Christian Religion and Church*, trans. Joseph Torrey (Boston: Crocker and Brewster, 1854), 191.

Chapter 8: Holy Subversion: The Birth of the Protestant Missionary Society

1. William Carey, *An Enquiry into the Obligation of Christians to Use Means for the Conversion of the Heathens* (Book Jungle, 2007).

Chapter 11: Indigenous Ingenuity: Church Planting in the Great Century

1. David B. Barrett and Todd Johnson, eds., *World Christian Trends, AD 30–AD 2200: Interpreting the Annual Christian Megacensus* (Pasadena, CA: William Carey Library, 2001), 24–33, 390–92.

Chapter 12: Global Collaboration: The Birth of World Christianity

1. W. H. Gairdner, *Edinburgh 2010: An Account and Interpretation of the World Missionary Conference* (Edinburgh: Oliphant, Anderson and Ferrier, 1910), 48–49.

Chapter 13: Pentecostalism in Latin America

1. William G. McLoughlin and Robert Bellah, eds., *Religion in America* (Boston: Houghton Mifflin, 1968), 47.

Chapter 14: The African Indigenous Churches in Sub-Saharan Africa

1. Philip Jenkins, *The Next Christendom: The Coming of Global Christianity* (Oxford: Oxford University Press, 2002), 56.
2. Ibid., 58.

3. See the World Christian Database, www.worldchristiandata base.org.

Chapter 18: The Korean Missionary Movement

1. Steve Sang-Cheol Moon, "The Protestant Missionary Movement in Korea: Current Growth and Development," *International Bulletin of Missionary Research*, vol. 32., no. 2 (April 2008), 59.

Chapter 19: Post-Christendom European Christianity

1. Philip Jenkins, *The Next Christendom: The Coming of Global Christianity* (New York: Oxford University Press, 2002), 220.
2. Philip Jenkins, *God's Continent: Christianity, Islam, and Europe's Religious Crisis* (New York: Oxford University Press, 2007), 49.
3. Danny Kruger, "There's Plenty of Life Left in the Churches," *Telegraph* (October 13, 2005). The *Telegraph* is a major newspaper in the UK.
4. Address given by Archbishop George Carey in 2005 and accessed at www.gcarey.co.uk/Speeches/2005/BeaconsDay1.html.
5. Jenkins, *God's Continent*, 88–89.